Oxford University Press, Walton Street,
Oxford OX2 6DP

*Oxford New York Toronto Delhi Bombay
Calcutta Madras Karachi Petaling Jaya
Singapore Hong Kong Tokyo Nairobi Dar es
Salaam Cape Town Melbourne Auckland*

and associated companies in *Berlin Ibadan*

British Library Cataloguing in
Publication Data

Stobbs, William
    Good King Wenceslas
    I. Title
    823′.914 [J]

ISBN 0-19-279873-1

Printed in Hong Kong

WILLIAM  STOBBS

# Good King Wenceslas

**OXFORD UNIVERSITY PRESS**

Oxford  Toronto  Melbourne

Good King Wenceslas looked out,

On the Feast of Stephen,

When the snow lay round about,

Deep, and crisp, and even:

Brightly shone the moon that night,
    Though the frost was cruel,
When a poor man came in sight,
    Gath'ring winter fuel.

'Hither, page, and stand by me,
If thou know'st it, telling,
Yonder peasant, who is he?
Where and what his dwelling?'

'Sire, he lives a good league hence,
  Underneath the mountain,

Right against the forest fence,
By Saint Agnes' fountain.'

'Bring me flesh, and bring me wine
Bring me pine-logs hither:
Thou and I will see him dine,
When we bear them thither.'

Page and monarch, forth they went,
Forth they went together;
Through the rude wind's wild lament
And the bitter weather.

'Sire, the night is darker now,
  And the wind blows stronger;
Fails my heart, I know not how,
  I can go no longer.'

'Mark my footsteps, good my page;
Tread thou in them boldly:
Thou shalt find the winter's rage
Freeze thy blood less coldly.'

In his master's steps he trod,
    Where the snow lay dinted;
Heat was in the very sod
    Which the saint had printed.

Therefore, Christian men, be sure,
Wealth or rank possessing,
Ye who now will bless the poor,
Shall yourselves find blessing.